"BE UNSTOPPABLE BECAUSE YOU CAN"

Ki is your host

Endorsements

"Walk Tall is a well-thought-out book that effectively condenses valuable lessons on how to build your confidence with simple understandings. Carry this book with you and study it every day and you may find that you, too, are standing tall."

(Peggy McColl, New York Times Best Selling Author & Author of Savy Wisdom)

"As someone who have studied this type of belief system my whole life, even I learned much from this book. Walk Tall both goes into great dept of wisdom and still maintains a simplicity of execution. That is very difficult to accomplish. Amazing."

(Deb Birdsall, Author of Overcoming My Mother´s Addictions)

"Walk Tall should be in deck format, easy to carry with you in your pocket or handbag. An inspiring book that makes me want to take care of a lot of broken pieces in my life. I think I have a good confidence but I have so much more capacity to improve it. Also do a big cleaning in my surroundings would be good. An eye-opener, energy thief, there's plenty when I look around at my surroundings. Feeling a redeeming force, wants to go out and shout Tokwanda as Katy Bates does in the film Fried Green Tomatoes at Whistle stop Cafe, when she is about to free herself from anything that bothers her in her liberating development."

(Annlouise Welin)

"The book is written beautifully in offering simple, practical advice on healing the inner mind by understanding the cause and root of limiting beliefs and self sabotaging habits that block many from becoming happier, better versions of themselves. By reprogramming my mindset and the thoughts that plague me on a daily basis, I am more self aware to use every situation whether good or bad to my advantage. A must read for anyone who is seeking self love and happiness within themselves."

(Kim Walker)

"Me and my son really needed this....if you only knew."

(Yolanda McKenney)

"I enjoyed this book, this is definitely an inspiration to anyone, young or old. Not only is this book pleasant to read but taught me new concepts I hadn't learned before reading. One lesson from this book that impacted me the most was that you have to let go of whatever anger or guilt you have towards someone or something in order t obecome the person you want to be. The world can be what you create it to be, but only if you allow it. If you have been struggling wit hfinding confidence or inspiration, this is the book to read."

(Mary F. Rhodes)

"From start to finish, Walk Tall; Create YourOwn Confidence, in short, is powerful. Walk Tall teaches the power to have confidence in oneself. Thisbook is a journey to discover what it means to be confident, finding inspiration, and become someone better, someone you have always strived to be. The book highlights specific steps to find inspiration, such as identifying the goal you want to achieve and how to live with and achieve that goal. Personally, confidence is something

that I have been struggling with for years. Whether it be about finding the confidence to speak up for myself or even something as simple as being confident in front of others. After reading this book, I realized that once you learn to accept and love yourself, others will do the same. Realistically, no one can change themselves over night, yet Walk Tall gives all the steps and motivation to reach whatever that goal may be. I strongly recommend this book to anyone. It is detailed and easy to understand, as definitions and explanations are provided in the book. Even if you do not like to read, think of it as less of a book and more of a personal growth guide. Either way, Walk Tall will help you find the motivation and inspiration you didn't evenknow you had."

(Jhana Rhodes)

"Very proud of my daughter. She wrote a book that everyone can understand, focusing on difficult emotional issues that can be solved with simple, innovative down to Earth models. Very easy to read and inspiring. Everyone should read it."

(Gerda Bergman)

"A small yet useful book trying to teach a very valuable skill one should work on i.e. building self-confidence. Throughout the book, the author shares her stories about her lack of confidence and how she has overcome it and was able to rise above all since her childhood. So how the book will serve you? This book will help you to learn the following:

1. the importance of "now" which is the only time dimension we have access to. Rests are just your "thoughts".

2. How self-love affects your self-confidence.

3. What change in your shift in mindset, from negative to positive, can bring in your life.

4. Why the growth-oriented mind is a necessity for everyone.

5. The 4 stairs of confidence.

6. Useful strategies for you to build confidence and much more.

What did I like the most in this book?

The "confidence stair" author has shared in this book is something new I learned from this book.

Now the important question is: who should read this? I personally believe this book is a good one for beginners to start reading. The small size and useful knowledge make it perfect for beginners. But if you have already read many books on self-help then this might not be useful to you."

(Shiromani Kant, readerpreneur.in)

"This book is inspirational, and will help you achieve your goals, and be confident in doing so. Therefore, if you love yourself and surround yourself with the right people, thru self discovery, the sky is the limit. Also, I love the references to Albert Einstein."

(Paula Sapp)

"A well-written self-help book that helps you with strength and self-confidence. Ki is your host's book is fantastic and easy to read and filled with her own experiences and relevant quotes from Einstein. An important topic about living in the present, free of negative

thoughts. She shows the way attract the good life you want, through emotions and the strength of your thoughts. Highly recommended."

(Eva H. Hertel)

"The book Walk Tall is a fantastic little manual that I can take with me and get advice from whenever I wish and need. The models in the book are easily understandable and useful. The book does not contain a lot of padding, but is short and concise. Can highly recommend this book."

(Helena Brandt)

"I've been doing a lot of meditation to build confidence, but I still found new things in the book. The best part is that it is so easy to read that you can read it several times and get new thoughts every time. I highly recommend it, and especially for those who want something easily accessible within self-help."

(Gunmarie Persson)

"The book has a positive message and a very nice layout for looking at life in a new way. I like the Albert Einstein quotes, albeit there were a few of them and this seems like a really good book for someone wanting to better themselves. Overall, it is a good book!"

(Jacary Lundy)

"A great book! I don't like to read long books and a lot of text so this is perfect for me. The book gave me several new thoughts that make it easier for me to sort things in my life. Great! Read it!"

(Mikael Svensson)

"Walk Tall introduces a set of keys for start make impact inside-out to turn chapter and level-up. Its easy to relate to events and apply to start getting unstuck. I love the concept "act as if it already is". I believe Ki is your host use words to point out actionable concepts grounded in best practise. I wish I would have had access to this book when I was younger."

(Erika Brandt, Dreamovator @ Dreamovation.se)

"By describing how to build your self-confidence in a straightforward, vivid, and engaging way, Walk Tall becomes an excellent read for anyone who is looking to take control over their future. Walk Tall has an important message and leaves the reader filled with both empowerment and new energy."

(Michaela Hoernfeldt)

"Walk Tall by Ki is your host is the book to be. The book oozes confidence and probably is the best book for growth, development, anything like that. It speaks about the hardships and points in life where you might want to give up. But it gives courage and a positive light to what will come and how to succeed. I also love the stories. Ki is your host mentions about her life as the book goes on. It gives a nice warm feeling to the book as if you could relate to the stories. The quotes put in there by Albert Einstein gives it a great touch. It keeps the reader going and helps in the journey to confidence. I recommend this book to any and everyone. And to those who might need some guidance in their life."

(Gabbi Sneed)

WALK TALL

Create your own self-confidence

by
Ki is your host

Hasmark
PUBLISHING
INTERNATIONAL

Editor: Brad Green – brad@hasmarkpublishing.com
Cover Design: Anne Karklins – anne@hasmarkpublishing.com
Book Design: Amit Dey – amit@hasmarkpublishing.com

ISBN 13: 978-1-77482-042-1
ISBN 10: 1774820420

Table of Contents

Can we look confident when we are not?

Yes, we can. However, we have to want it, and we must learn how to feel it!

Much like planning the steps required to reach a goal, in the same way, you need to take certain steps to become confident—to *Walk Tall*!

When you look confident, other people will find you reliable and attractive, and they will trust you in most of life's situations. Think about how momentously you will benefit from that!

If you want it, you should get it!

And you can!

"If you never feel uncomfortable, then you are not serious about development. Walk Tall is a mini-book intended to be carried with you for daily use; it is all about developing your inner self to set you up for success in life."

Ki is your host (Kee) is a European marketing strategist, former musician and athlete, who has made it her mission to develop that which has not been done before. She has studied both markets and people all over the world, and created her own process to develop self-confidence and strategic thinking.

Acknowledgements

An inspired thank you to my mentor, Peggy McColl, *New York Times* Best-selling Author, for a wonderful atmosphere and learning experience.

A warm thank you also to my beautiful friends, Bryant Sapp and Gunmarie Persson, who have inspired me to write this book, and especially to Bryant for "walking tall." A special thank you to Mikael Svensson for your tireless support.

Much love, guys!

Chapter One

Get Rid of What Does Not Serve You!

What a wonderful day!

And here I am. I fly forward with every step I take!

I move rhythmically across the ground while I humbly and happily greet the people around me.

I am comfortable in myself; I feel happy on my way to the meeting, and I am excited! Regardless of the outcome, I am safe, I am prepared, and know that I can handle any situation. It's even fun to stand in front of an audience and talk!

And am I not a little beautiful too?

Anyone who wants to can decide to become confident, and I will share with you exactly how to proceed, step by step. It's surprisingly simple. All you have to do is practice these steps and implement them into your daily life.

Everything comes from within us!

How we think and feel determines how others look at us!

And this is where things often go wrong. What others think of us does not matter; I do not need anyone's approval. It does not serve me to let other people determine how I should feel in any way. But the thing is, if I allow them to be involved, they certainly will!

And if that happens, I am completely under the control of their thoughts, and not my own!

Do you understand? Do you want other people's values to control how you feel? I should hope not.

All situations are neutral from the beginning. I determine their value and decide how I should relate to each situation. I also decide for myself how I should relate to what others think.

It's entirely my own fault if I let situations and people control how I feel. It's not their business to crawl into my body and disturb my thoughts, so I have to decide for myself that what they think about me actually has nothing to do with me at all. They can think what they want; it's their thought—not mine.

I choose how I want to think and feel.

Wouldn't that be super nice?

Wouldn't it feel nice to decide for yourself how you should feel in any situation, and know that no matter what, you are safe and confident?

It's a lovely and warm feeling.

So…I walk here and fly lightly on my feet on this wonderful day! Checking out nice guys in the sunshine and daring to smile at anyone—yes, this is me!

But that was not always the case.

When I was growing up, I was a small, cool girl who played music, sang, and stood on stage during national live broadcasts at only nine years old. But later, my middle school and primary school years were not as fun. The girls in my class did everything they could to bring me down to earth, while I mostly hung out with the boys. Sometimes I sat alone in the girls' locker room after gym class and wished I had enough self-confidence to just jump into the popular group and hang out with them. These were probably the only years in my life that I felt a little nauseous. I was expelled from the girl's group because they did not like the fact that I was the one leading the theater group, that I was the one on three of our school's sports teams, that I was the one who wrote short stories that were published, and attended a music school that would lead me to the rock scene.

Finishing primary school was liberating, and I could continue with sports and music and become as good as I wanted without feeling uncomfortable because I was "too good" among those who would be my "friends." They also made me dislike school.

You can be frozen out for several reasons. Jealousy can cause anyone to lose self-confidence, and this is as common in the adult world as it is in the world of school children. Often, it is adults who are insecure, who seek strength in pushing someone else down. As soon as you see that behavior, you can take comfort in the fact that their self-confidence must be totally below water level.

Unfortunately, it is still the case that when several people look at you a certain way at the same time, their opinion or judgement can suddenly become a reality. But this is true *only* if you allow them to decide for you how to look at the situation.

Do not become one of them, because by doing so, you will become your own enemy! It is up to you to decide how to look at the situation!

So, how did I get out of my discomfort then?

> *"In the middle of difficulty lies opportunity."*
>
> — Albert Einstein

I was only 14 years old, and a little too young to understand everything as I do today. I found my way out by being successful in what I did, being the one that people applauded and watched—and the one that they respected—because I was good at several things. By becoming good at something, you can gain respect. However, gaining respect does not always mean that you will gain confidence in every situation.

It is not always how you look or what you do that determines how others see you. It is often, for the most part, a lack of the psychological impact that you could have on your surroundings. It is the way you radiate.

How can I affect my surroundings psychologically? How can I radiate?

You do this from within, through the image that you create of yourself. Even if you do not think this is possible, it is. You are free to create the image you want for yourself; you can believe in it and follow it. That is true for you, and it's true for me too.

Think about the many artists and inventors who at first were not believed in by others, who were laughed at, but who believed so much in themselves that they ultimately began to convince others to believe in them as well.

It is crucial to believe in yourself and what you do if you want to move forward, and if you want to feel good. Pushing things away because you are intimidated or because you don't feel safe characterizes your path through life and puts limits on your capabilities. If you are insecure and afraid, you can either continue to be so, or you can obtain the tools needed to train yourself to believe in yourself. When you change, the world around you also begins to change in a magical way.

I know, it sounds incredible. But when your charisma changes, you also get a different response from the rest of the world. You will see it!

Your charisma and your energy mean that you are automatically connected to people and places with the same energy. That is, what you give, you get back. That's why it all starts with you!

This book can help you find and utilize the tools that make building confidence much easier, and it opens doors. Radiating insecurity also makes others around you insecure. They first become insecure about you, and that insecurity spreads to the entire situation. In this way, insecure people are attracted to you. These are not the positive and attractive people you would like to surround yourself with.

As I mentioned, there are several different kinds of poor self-confidence. You can be very good at one thing, while at the same time, feel very insecure about another.

I had a friend at school who was very quiet among his friends, but a giant on the basketball court. He directed and controlled the entire team from his guard position with a loud voice, gestures and three-point shots. He had his own fan club of girls from other classes—those who only saw him on the court. In the schoolyard, he was barely visible. If any of us girls addressed him outside the basketball court, it was almost as if he would become scared and run away.

I have been thinking about that.

This idea that you can be so attractive in one situation, but yet so bland in another, all comes back to charisma. It comes down to your image. When you believe in yourself, you become almost like another human being, and you feel good!

Is it not amazing that I can have this influence on myself?

So…what are you waiting for?

Signed, sealed, and delivered! Here we go!

It's also common to be unsure about something that stems from being treated a certain way. In the end, it is still me and my inner self that will decide how I should approach that situation.

At the end of this book, I will share a strengthening process that has worked on several of my friends, as well as people I have met from around the world. This process has also worked for the youths I have trained to reach elite levels in various sports, as well as for business leaders. Last but not least, it has worked for me. This is firsthand knowledge being distributed here.

Are you ready to begin the journey towards building self-confidence and having an attractive image? Are you ready to change your life?

Of course you are!

The journey begins with yourself, and it begins now.

You need to start from scratch (zero). You cannot start by being burdened with negative thoughts. The first thing you need to do is let go of the things that are dragging you down. You need to let go of what no longer serves you, and what you do not feel good about. Throw it away! These negativities gnaw at you, and tend to come back easily. The basis of self-confidence is to start from scratch where you are free, so that you are not eaten up by bad memories or negative thoughts.

The first step towards self-confidence is to become free. When you've become free, you can also deal with the negative attacks that you encounter in life.

How do you become free? By getting rid of negativity.

However, it is not so easy to get rid of your own negative thoughts. It is in your thoughts that everything is built up or broken down. You can make an active decision in how you want to approach different situations, and what you put into them. You need to first get rid of what drags you down, and then learn what tools to use to deal with negative attacks from the outside—those things that you do not benefit from.

Start by dividing your negativity into groups. Feel free to list them as I have:

1. The past
2. The present
3. The future

It's important to be fully aware of what you need to include in these groups. Is there something from your past that hurts or hinders you? Are there people or things in your life today that make you uncomfortable? Is there something that you are afraid will happen to you in the future?

You need to identify what makes you uncomfortable and become aware of it. You cannot remove something if you are unaware of its existence.

Let us start with the past.

We all have things that haunt us and prevent us from optimizing our performance. These things show up from time to time, and we may back off, feel depressed, feel regret, or develop a bad feeling. It is robbing us of energy because we come back to it over and over again. Do you recognize it? You are not alone. This is very common.

But do you know what the best thing is?

You can change all this by yourself!

It is quite possible to let go of the past no matter how serious the trauma or how serious the events are that you have been through. It could be breakups, deaths, loss of businesses, abuse, health problems, bullying, accidents, or anything else that has remained inside of you.

You can change this. It is human psychology. But the question is, do you want to change it? You must want to change it! You will need to create an entirely new emotional plan, and re-evaluate how you think about and view things.

> *"I must be willing to give up who I am, in order to become what I will be."*
>
> — Albert Einstein

To begin with, you need to understand that the past is a project, or an event. It is not real because it does not exist here and now. It was real before, but now it no longer exists. It may feel real to you, and it may be difficult to let go of, but consider carefully: *the past does not exist; it is only in your thoughts.*

The future is also a project (or event). Like the past, it does not exist here and now. The only thing that exists and that is real is the here and now, this minute. Even the future only exists in your thoughts. The only thing that exists is the "here and now" – everything else is only a thought in your mind. The past is a thought. The future is a thought. So if you can control your thoughts, you can change the meaning of the past and the future.

Putting too much emotional charge into something that does not exist is not necessary. Our thoughts about the past and the future, therefore, need to be limited to only that which benefits us; we must let go of what does not serve us.

What you think is real from the past is only real in your mind.

What you think will happen tomorrow is still a project, because it does not yet exist. This means that you can still shape it. This is a fantastic opportunity! You do not really know what will happen tomorrow, so you can see it as a blank canvas and plan to paint it with good and colorful things. Do not dismiss strategy or critical thinking. Use your thoughts to strengthen the strategy that benefits you.

You may have to go through this a few times. For many, it is new to think that only the present exists. But if you think about it, it is true. So, get into the now, get into the moment, get into what is real. Stop thinking about the past and the future. It is *now* that matters; everything else is only a project that does not exist in the present.

If you do not let go of the past, you will keep allowing negative thoughts inside, and your energy will be occupied by these negativities. The good stuff will be squeezed out. Understand that the past only exists because you are allowing it to. If you did not, it would not remain because it does not exist. Just let it go. Decide to let it go and stop thinking about it.

How about the present? What did you put on your list?

Are there situations that worry you? Are you worried about what others say about you, or what they might say to you? Is it the feeling of being outside the group? Have you experienced something worrying? Maybe a breakup?

All people are energy. Both people and things vibrate on different frequencies. Just as mobile phones communicate on frequencies, human energy does the same thing. There's really nothing strange about it. Maybe we do not think about this so often, and therefore do not understand how we can use this energy to our advantage. If we feel down and out, we vibrate on a frequency where we meet like-minded people. The same applies if we feel strong and inspired. If we radiate this positivity, we will attract like-minded people; we will attract those who communicate on the same frequency.

It is important to sort your thoughts in the "now" section so that you can observe them, identify them, and let go of any that do not serve you. You need to be aware of what thoughts to look for and let them go. I think it is easier to list everything I think about in the "now." By doing so, I can easily identify the negative ones that I should get rid of. The more negative thoughts you let go of, the easier you feel in your mind. It's a "training thing" to let go, but the more you train, the better you get at it and the higher you fly!

So, let go of your guilt, anger, or regret! Forgive yourself and forgive others!

First, be aware of what this thought is and allow it to be there. Watch it from a neutral perspective, and then allow yourself to let it go. You don´t need it. Realize that people will always make choices out of their own level of ratio-nalization and their own perspectives, and they might not see it the way you do. So…accept and forgive, and let it go!

Feeling free and raising your own vibration is the result of letting go of negativity. It's easier to no longer have to carry around negative energy. It's too heavy a load!

The key to freedom is letting go, because everything resides in your thoughts. Let the thoughts be there, observe them from a neutral place, and then let them go. Allow your feelings to appear, observe them, and then let them go.

Let it all go!

Every situation is neutral with no built-in meaning. We choose the meaning we get from the situations in life.

Yes, it is a choice!

Something that both myself and people around me have noticed is that our entire environment will respond in a completely new way, and we will come to see it differently.

I had been training to let go for six months when I saw more clearly the changes that had slowly but surely crept up on me. It was a wonderful feeling to suddenly see the world with different eyes. But it was not the world that had changed, it was me! And I changed the way my world looked at me! I suddenly found myself in another frequency where I attracted people with positive energy because I was positive.

It cannot get better, believe me!

And all I had to learn was to *let go*!

"The world as we have created it is a process of our thinking. It cannot be changed without changing our thinking."

— Albert Einstein

Chapter Two

Releasing Attachment

Let's keep talking about the now.

Get the vacuum cleaner out so we can clean up your interior!

After a general cleaning, we will rebuild and become even stronger. To let go of negativities and really live here and now and feel free is the whole basis for stable self-confidence. Negative attachments are the cause of most of our suffering. This is an attachment to belief systems, to how people are, to thoughts, and to viewing yourself in a certain way. You must let go of the notion that "I am this person," and instead believe that you can get exactly where you want to go. Do not be afraid. Results will come with less effort.

The release of an attachment is the release of the meaning we have created around this attachment. Anything you are attached to has a meaning. You might think that you are attached to a person, but you are not. Rather, you are attached to what that person means to you. That meaning is what you have been thinking about, and what you have decided this person should mean with regards to your life. It's your decision.

In another example, you may also be attached to a job and see it as your identity. Again, it is you who has decided to give this attachment its meaning. It is not the job itself, but rather the attachment to it and what it means to you that you constantly direct your thoughts towards.

There are several different types of attachments, and it can be difficult to rid yourself of them because it is difficult to let go of your thoughts. In order to do so, you must also let go of the outcome. The outcome does not matter; whatever happens will happen. You are prepared for all different outcomes, much like strategic thinking. How a certain situation goes does not matter because you are prepared.

> *"To dwell on the things that depress or anger us does not help in overcoming them. One must knock them down alone."*
>
> — Albert Einstein

What exactly is release of attachment?

It is release of the meaning, and that meaning is created by your own thoughts. We give things their meaning; it is of our own doing.

Do you now understand how much your thoughts mean?

You can look at it from different perspectives and decide what meaning each situation or person should have in your life or your day. When you think that something must work out in a certain way, you create resistance, which can lead to a feeling of desperation. When you focus your thoughts on something happening just the way you want it to, it will be felt by the outer world as desperate energy. This will immediately come back to you because humans (and the universe) will perceive you as a person who is missing something. That is not attractive.

Attachment within you creates resistance that is reflected back on you when your ego wants to create certainty. The more you let go, the freer you will feel, and the more positivity will come back to you. It works 100% of the time.

Do not misunderstand this, though. When it comes to strategic planning and a company that sets up deliverables, you need to calculate outcomes and coat them with goals that you are working towards. This should, of course, be done in a positive spirit where a positive charge is reflected towards the outside world.

This also applies to your own personal goals, because you need goals to secure your direction. I have noticed that people become happier, and even more positive, when they work towards goals. A person can have both personal and professional goals. When it comes to becoming confident, you can set very personal goals related to your thoughts and behaviors.

I think that goals help because people need to be disciplined when they are learning how to think differently. You have to "feed yourself" with new thoughts and do it continuously. Goals help us stay on track and move in the right direction, and moving in the right direction is always an important thing to do.

Below are different types of attachments. See if you recognize yourself in any of these. You can also say that attachment is an approach that you decide on yourself.

I have listed four attachment types:

CONFIDENT: Not afraid of being open and vulnerable, relaxed, confident, dares to set goals and work towards them without focusing all their attention on the outcome. Follows a natural "life flow."

ANXIOUS: Must know the outcome because the outcome means everything. Seeks validation, leans in, and will try to impact the direction towards the outcome he or she would like to have happen.

RESISTING: Afraid of deeper relationships, constantly holding back, resisting confrontation, has trust issues, and has an attitude of avoiding many situations.

NEUTRAL: Careless and unaware of their surroundings, makes mistakes, but does not really care about them. This person simply exists, but takes no action, whether positive or negative.

You attract the qualities that you radiate. These four types will attract back exactly the energy that they radiate out. The confident personality fills up his or her own cup and does not need validation from anyone else, but is still open and secure in a way that attracts other successful and "like-minded" people. By "life flow," I mean to casually follow the flow of opportunities and people who are attracted to your positive openness. A flow is created when positive vibes meet at the same frequency. Let things happen and learn to see the possibilities with an open mind.

You need to be aware of your attachment style in order to be able to change it. You cannot influence that which you are not aware of. Awareness is always key. There are so many unaware people around us, which is very unfortunate. These people do not know how to change their life in the direction they want it to go, and they don't know that the only thing they have to do is direct their thoughts towards another target.

> *"We cannot solve our problems with the same level of thinking that created them."*
>
> — Albert Einstein

We are whole and complete. We are the finest creation of energy. However, when we attach ourselves to someone else and let them become our source of validation, so much so that we feel incomplete without them, then we will always lack something within ourselves. As a result, we will attract people who are not whole and complete. These people might carry all sorts of things with them that can bring us down because they lack something themselves and will attract more of the same.

The confident person has told himself or herself that he is whole and complete. His or her thoughts are directed towards inner fullness in all aspects, and this will attract the same in a potential partner. The person we love and who will love us is supposed to enrich our lives, not create dependence. In this case, love can be free, happy, and deep.

Most of the things you are attached to will create some type of suffering when someone is not acting the way you want, when someone is not showing you the validation you seek, or when some type of outcome is not the outcome you wanted or expected.

To build lasting self-confidence, you need to be free inside. Do you understand how I think here?

If something weighs on you inside, it will drag you down. So it is important that you do the job properly from the ground up. You will succeed if you do.

"Meaning" is the biggest part of this, because we decide what things mean to us. We think about these things, and their meaning is shaped by our thoughts. That is also why we can reshape ourselves. Let go of the meaning. The meaning gives all the power and energy to the situation or to the person to whom you give this meaning. That puts you in a position of needing. If you don´t give the person a meaning that serves you well, you will end up needing them. So, it's all about our minds and the meaning we give things. Human beings are naturally "unconditional love." It is how we handle attachment that creates the resistance.

Let go of meaning—create your own.

Give yourself the meaning of being whole and complete. The key to releasing the past is releasing the meaning and reframing it. Remember, it is your thoughts that determine this. Let that person go with love. Don´t keep a negative charge, because then you will only attract more negativity.

Some of my friends are waiting to meet the right one… prince charming or princess charming. They spend valuable time longing and thinking about what will happen when they finally meet. They are attached to the outcome, and as a result, they are not happy with where they are today. They are not whole and complete, and they will attract the same because of the signals they send out.

One of my friends wondered why she attracted the same kind of men every time. "I'm never lucky in love," she said. "Every single person I meet has a problem that is so serious that the relationship ends…and I'm left alone again! Always alone!"

If you see yourself as "always alone," it's probably because this is the energy that you radiate when you meet someone new. You almost expect "your usual bad luck" to occur. Instead, ask yourself why you always attract the same type of partners, and why you are "looking for" them. A person who is "always lonely" might not be as attractive as a person who shines "whole and complete."

Don´t you think?

Don't wait. Change your perspective and the world around you will change. That is 100% given. When you are whole and complete, this energy will radiate to the outer world and you will attract someone who is the same, someone who can bring happiness into your life. Someone who can be an addition to your already complete self. Your energy will become attractive because you know you are attractive! You attract the same, that is so true. Your thoughts make all the difference.

Two people who are attached to the same situation can give the situation completely different meanings, and therefore get completely different results. Two people on the same path can end up in different locations in life. It is more important than we sometimes understand to be able to see situations from a perspective that serves us. And again, it starts with our own thoughts.

Can people look confident even though they are not?

The truth is in the eye of the beholder, so it is your audience you have to convince. But you cannot convince the audience to believe if you are not a believer yourself. This process that I am giving you works; you just need to put in the daily effort and stay committed.

"You never fail until you stop trying."

— Albert Einstein

There are often mental obstacles that attempt to block us when trying something that we have never tried before. Trying to "think right" can seem difficult when you are unsure of what to do. For me, it was difficult in the beginning. And I'm sure it will be the same for you. But when you really get into the exercises, the more time you spend working on this, the easier it will become. Your thoughts are your strongest weapon. Thoughts are stronger than anything else, so it is your thoughts that you need to practice changing.

"The measure of intelligence is the ability to change."

— Albert Einstein

I think it's exciting to do something that I've never done before. It's exciting to find out what's around the corner. What happens if I connect new things to each other, and so on? But I can promise that I was ready to vomit in the beginning, when I was thrown out from one of the towers of the military academy, covered with a hood, immediately after an interrogation. Yes, that is what happened when I took the exam in leadership. I was on unknown ground with people I had never met!

A great exercise!

Every time you throw yourself out there, it goes better and better. Now, this has become something that I often do and that I see as developing me. (Well, not from the towers at the military academy, but from other kinds of towers.) The more you do one thing, the better it goes. And each time, you become more open-minded. All I can say is this: never stop throwing yourself out, because the future gains are huge!

I do not care what others think about what I do, because I do not need their approval. My mind is stronger than theirs, and I control this myself! I do not intend to unite with the enemy and engage in any self-sabotage!

How about that!

Remember, all thoughts and beliefs come from inside of us.

Fear can prevent us from moving forward. Remember, it is how we choose to look at things that affects this. There are people who are scared and protect themselves by having an attitude. I usually look back at the girls from my days in school who really had an attitude when they froze me out of the group. I can smile at that today, and think that it was an excellent experience to refer to in this book. I also wonder how it went for these girls later in life.

How we see situations depends on, as we have talked about, how aware we are of ourselves and our surroundings. Often, you do not understand how to get there and may need a structure to "go through" yourself.

I have put together a model that has worked well for myself and others. I suggest you write your own answers under the headings below.

Model by Ki is your host.

To the right in the image, we see our own interior. And to the left, we see the profile that we want to give out to the world.

Approaching Mind = The conscious mind. Decides what we should take in, assesses situations, and is active in making decisions. The Approaching Mind can also focus and direct your thoughts towards different things, and here you can decide how this should go. It is important that you use this ability to control your thoughts and actively choose how to look at situations. Here you can make sure that negative things do not get in and you can let go of what does not serve you.

Write down what you want in your life, as well as what you do not want and actively follow this.

The Master Mind = The subconscious mind. It does not sort or choose; it receives everything that is let in by the Approaching Mind. In addition, this space is a warehouse for memories and events from earlier in life, those that can have a serious effect on you if they are negative or difficult. If you do not identify them and make efforts to rid yourself of them, these negative things can reduce your self-confidence and ability to perform. You may need to list who or what they are in order to view them, and then to be able to let them go. In order for them to disappear, you need to replace them with something else, which means that you need to re-program yourself.

Decision Edging = Making the best and sharpest decisions. This occurs when you actively triangulate a holistic view of your surroundings and connect selected factors to create new, successful scenarios that you make decisions against. I have created this many times for businesses, but it also works great for people who want to get better at making decisions and making appropriate connections between opportunities in their life.

Programs = We are programmed since birth. These programs are stored in The Master Mind. If these programs do not serve us because they are painful, disturb us, or are otherwise not good for us, we must rid ourselves of them. They could be bad memories that haunt us, or a variety of other things that place limits on us. To get rid of them, we have to replace them with new programs. In order for the new program to push out the old one, we need to rehearse the new program daily and give it the power of thought.

That which we focus on becomes our reality.

For example, if we have been in an accident and experience it over and over again, we need to shift focus to that fantastic goal we want to achieve next year. We must live in the goal as if it has already been achieved, see ourselves there, and constantly focus on the wonderful feeling that the target has already been reached. The more we repeat this thought process, the weaker grip the negative thoughts will have on us, and this is how our mind works. Most important of all is the sensation that comes with really *feeling* that we are "living in the goal." In order for programs to be replaced, you need to live in—and feel—the new program throughout your entire body.

Yes, developing this capability is also a "training thing" that requires endurance, but it works 100% if you decide to go for it.

Consequences = All decisions have consequences, and these need to be dealt with, positive and negative. How many times have you thought, "Why did I do this? Now look what's happened," or, "How lucky I was to have done this. Otherwise, this would not have happened to me."

It is important to look at the consequence and see what is positive in this context. The funny thing is that you can always find something positive, even in the most negative of situations. You have to be open. Feeling good and seeing the positive in things is an approach that changes lives.

Now, let's look at the left side of the image where you can see "Cake and Edge" – this is about image and pro-filing. Even if you build up your inner strength, there will still be ups and downs in life for us to deal with. You will find yourself in situations where you want to appear confident when you are not. Is this possible? Yes. Absolutely. If you have a good foundation—if you have learned to control your thoughts—you can also control them on a "bad day," because you built up the collection of tools to do so.

I remember one day when I was going to give a talk to a group of managers from various industries. I woke up with a bad cold, and I almost panicked because this lecture was very important. I remember my white face with red eyes, and my rosy, red nose staring back at me in the mirror. I felt awful. I looked like a clown!

In a situation like this, it is simply not possible to wait for the uncertainty to take over. In this situation, "attack mode" is the best defense. I must take command immediately!

I woke up my Approaching Mind and decided then and there, as I looked in that mirror, that this would be one of my best days ever. I let go of the feeling of being sick, loaded myself up with throat lozenges and handkerchiefs, put eye drops in my eyes, and powdered my face so that no one could see my clown nose. I placed myself in the starting blocks and quickly handled everything.

It was my best day!

It was a perfect day!

During the lecture, I accidentally coughed a throat lozenge out of my mouth. It flew straight out towards the audience while I continued to talk! They smiled politely, but I was so focused on my speech that I had no room for embarrassment. And guess what? This became one of my best performances! Why? Because I had already decided that it was going to be so before I left my home that day!

When I returned home, I was completely knocked out and fell into bed. But that's a different story.

By word and by action, I have built my profile as being a leader who delivers, and being a person who my business partners can fully trust. I will fight until the end. Among my friends, I am the one you come to for advice and support, because they know that my mind is as open as the entire universe. And what do we know about the universe? It is infinite.

Do not expect to get "timid" advice from me. No…I am a challenger and innovator who constantly wants to push the boundaries, and this is an intentional part of my image. I own both my successes and failures. You know what you get with me, and people like to know what they're getting.

Building an image takes time, and you need to decide how you want the environment to perceive you. Then, you must work actively to achieve it, regardless of whether you're having a good or bad day. When you have such a direction, you can easily handle those moments when you do not feel confident because you have developed a technique for handling that situation. You must keep moving forward no matter how you feel on any given day.

Model by Ki is your host.

To the left in the image, you can see the figure for Cake and Edge.

EDGE = Your profiling towards the outside world that will attract those who you want to reach or need to reach. It's like embedding value in a brand by combining what the recipient is attracted to with your own delivery. This is where you give the promise of your delivery, and what you offer as a person, participant, leader, or friend.

CAKE = This is your delivery, your content, your work, and what will strengthen your "edge." If you do not deliver what you profiled outwardly, the environment will feel cheated and will not trust you again. The same applies (but conversely), if the "edge" is not attractive enough, or was put together the wrong way. No one will ever know what your "cake" looks like because they will not be interested.

"Edge" is charisma and image, meaning that being confident is part of your concept. Therefore, the "edge" needs to be "you" and not something that the outside world wants you to be. Be genuine. You are who you are. If you list your qualities, you will find several things that you can profile and strengthen. You will find things that make the environment around you perceive you in a certain way—the way you want to be perceived.

Self-confidence is based on the values that you radiate in your "edge." So, it is mainly about being yourself and finding your advantages. Self-confidence will increase automatically if you reinforce the things you are already good at. If you reinforce the things you aren't good at by trying to lift them to the zero line, you will not get an "edge" at all. "Edge" means that something stands out, is reinforced, and visible. So again, in order to create a strong and present profile in your environment, you must choose something that you are good at, and then work to reinforce it.

I often hear voices saying, "I'm not good at anything special." But nothing could be further from the truth. Not long ago, I talked to a friend. "What am I good at?" he asked. He then answered himself: "Nothing." I thought this was strange, and I asked him to list all the things he did in his daily life. He did so, then read the list to me. I saw it at once!

It was very clear that he was good at communicating and building relationships face to face. All these conversations had ended in his favor. I pointed out that he was an excellent communicator, that he showed great strength in how he communicated during meetings with people. He listened in silence. After a while, he replied, "You are right. I always get where I want to go in meetings. My communication is a strength!"

Sometimes there can be small details that you do not value, but that can mean an enormous amount in a person's image to the outside world. Strengths can be practically anything. It could be something you are good at but which you have not yet tried, or something else. Everyone has strengths!

What are your strengths?

> *"Everybody is a genius. But if you judge a fish by its ability to climb a tree it will live its whole life believing that it is stupid."*
>
> — Albert Einstein

Chapter Three

Radiation and Love

Love is a strong force. It is electrified, and it is so powerful that if we learn to channel this energy, there is no one who can stop us. When we channel and focus our thoughts, the strength of our thoughts is enormous.

What your thoughts are focused on is what you will feel.

What you feel will impact your decisions.

Your decisions will impact your path in life.

Your thoughts are the substance of what you radiate out into the world, and therefore your thoughts are the substance of how people see you.

Your thoughts can change your life.

Self-confidence is linked to self-love. Bring love to yourself, and you will have heaps of love to offer to others. A whole and complete person attracts other whole and complete people, because whole and complete people will find themselves in the same space and on the same frequency.

You create resistance by missing things, or by focusing on how much you miss that thing. You need to re-program yourself into being whole and complete, into feeling good about being whole and complete, and trusting that your heart will lead you where you need to go. And your heart will lead you, because it is supported by the energy of the universe. This is the energy that will align with the energy of your soulmate the moment you enter the same frequency. So you need to be "in" that energy and to "live" in that situation in heart and soul to physically be able to get there!

It is your positive thoughts that guide you to that place, and that attract new people to you. You will feel this energy of love flowing through you when you have confidence.

Allow the natural law of attraction to take place: what you send out will come back to you. The man or woman you want will not be interested in a gloomy figure—you have to radiate positivity!

You have to learn that similar energies attract each other, and that is part of the process. Also, the more we love ourselves, the more we can love others, and they will love us in return.

You will be worth loving!

The relationships we have will expand or fade away, and both experiences serve our higher good. We must let go of what does not serve us; this is an absolute must.

Sometimes we actually see the "red flags," and without really putting the finger on it, we understand that the person we are interested in may not be on the same frequency as us. Their energy may not be positive, or they may simply not be open enough, but it is just a gut feeling that we have. Most of us think that we can change the other person, but this is only possible if the other person wants to change themself. We believe that love overcomes all, but it becomes difficult if the other person's thoughts do not match the direction in which we are heading, or they lack what is needed to reach the atmosphere where our happiness exists.

Success in all relationships starts with success in the relationship we have with the "self." You need a great deal of awareness, self-responsibility, self-discipline, self-understanding, self-compassion, and self-respect. That is, if you are confident in yourself, you can lay the foundation for a happy relationship. You will also find it easier to identify an imaginary partner who is on the same frequency as you. Likewise, you will more easily identify when the person is not on the same frequency.

The more responsible we are with "self"—be it our finances, self-nurture, exercise, food, nutrition, careers, et cetera—the more respected we will be in all areas, and the more beautiful our relationships with others will be. If we want respect from others, we must first truly respect ourselves and let that respect shine through.

Are you taking care of yourself?

Your Master Mind must understand that you deserve to be loved and store that feeling inside.

You remember our storage space, don´t you?

To not feel worthy of love is just a paradigm that you must rid yourself of because it does not serve you. Let it go!

To always "pick the wrong partner" is yet another paradigm that must go. These mismatches are about frequencies—but yes, your "gut feeling" is part of that.

The law of attraction works in every aspect of our lives. What we radiate out is what we receive back to ourselves. And so it is with love. But to succeed in obtaining this wonderful return of attraction and happiness, it is necessary that we already *FEEL* this way, that we live in the situation that we desire, that we see this situation as a truth in the here and now. We need to capture that feeling. To help you do this, try dividing it into three steps.

1. **Identify the feeling**: What are the situations you want to be in, and how does this feel? What kind of feeling do you desire?

2. **Establish the feeling**: When you know how you want to feel, you need to establish this feeling within yourself. Take in the feeling, and know that it is possible. Accept it.

3. **Practice the feeling**: After acceptance, you should live in this feeling, and feel it as if it were already

here. The feeling is crucial for your radiation, and thus for how you will succeed in getting back the energy that you radiate out. Close your eyes. Meditate. Talk to yourself and act as if you are already living in the feeling of the situation you desire. Everything you wished for is already here, and you can live in it!

If you can perfect this mental practice, I can assure you that it is only a matter of time before the situation you imagine becomes a reality! The stronger we feel, the faster this will become a reality. Yes, I know that it is so because many of us practice these positive thoughts and are succeeding, living in their reality now. You attract what you are.

This same practice is efficient when running a business. You need to make most decisions as if you are already living in the future scenario. Otherwise, you will not adapt your business in the direction that you want it to go. You will only adapt it to the current situation, and then nothing will change. You may even miss opportunities for new development.

This is true in any situation—in love, business, other relationships, and life in general. It's not hocus pocus or weird in any way, it's really just common sense. What you radiate out into the world will radiate back to you.

A friendly smile is answered with a friendly smile.

If the image you see today does not match the image you want for your future, you must change the image in your mind to make a change in your reality. You have to start living in the new image and make decisions as if you are already living in it. If you do, you will inevitably get there.

Make sense?

Oh, yes!

Chapter Four

Understanding Change – and Using It!

"It cannot be changed without changing our thinking.
If the facts don't fit the theory, change the facts."

— Albert Einstein

Change can make you stronger!

There is one thing we can always be sure of in this life, and that is the presence of change. Change will always be there and is constantly happening, even though many people are afraid of it and do not want to accept it so easily.

We can also be sure about all the opportunities that come from change. If we are open to change, we are also open to the new opportunities that can mean so very much to us.

Isn't it absolutely wonderful that new opportunities are constantly emerging as a result of changes that are happening around us? There is something positive in every change, even a disaster, and it is important that we are attentive to this. Working against change is the worst thing you can do, and it also underscores low self-esteem.

Why work against something that you cannot change when you could be taking advantage of it instead? The greatest opportunities come from changes that take place in the outside world. Take a step back and when change occurs, observe it, and identify any gaps or benefits that may arise from it. You will find them. They may appear in completely different arenas as a consequence of the change, but the benefits will be there waiting for you.

Why am I talking about change?

Well…because it is important!

Those who have worked with themselves to improve their own self-confidence will be able to better use the benefits that come with change. Confidence will be present in every aspect of your life, and will make your life better.

Similar to how an athlete trains their body to a high level, you can train your awareness to a high level and build yourself up little by little. And just like how athletes often must endure injuries or take falls, so will you. But now, your falls will not be as impactful as those who are completely untrained. A completely untrained person can fall straight through all safety nets to the bottom! It's a psychological crash. But…I have good news!

Such a crash can mostly be avoided if we build our inner self stronger and train ourselves daily by using simple tools that we can implement in our lives.

Below you can see The Confidence Stairs. I have created this model to describe your path from survival to confidence. Maybe you are already in step two: establishment. Each person must determine for themselves which step they are currently standing on.

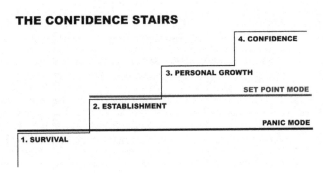

THE CONFIDENCE STAIRS

Model by Ki is your host.

The main purpose of the stair model is, of course, not simply to be a staircase. It is, rather, to highlight the importance of evaluating your inner self—your Master Mind and your Approaching Mind—to build your confidence step by step so that you can manage stress and make better decisions when you encounter stress or difficult situations in your life.

The steps of the stairs contain the following:

1. **Survival**: On this step, we think only of survival. Eating, sleeping, coping with the day—existing. This mainly relates to people in crisis or other difficulties, as well as newborn children, which means that we all start here.

2. **Establishment**: On this step, you have established for yourself the most important things you need for a good life. These things could be comfortable housing, a good job, hobbies, and maybe a partner. Many people choose to stay here on this step. This may be because they are not brave enough, are not mentally open, or simply do not understand what great value they could further add to their lives and how much happier and prosperous they could be. And there are those who want to move further, but simply do not know how.

3. **Personal Growth**: It is on this step that the most crucial development takes place. Unfortunately, as I said, there are far too few people here. Only those who have a higher degree of awareness will land here.

   Are you on the Personal Growth step? This step is fantastic!

   This is where we start with our inner development. Since you are reading this book right now, you are likely engaged in this practice of inner development on the Personal Growth step. On this step, there are people who seek development and who actively want to improve themselves personally, their lives in general, and their opportunities. It is a very positive step—and fun!

4. **Confidence**: The work executed on the third step (Personal Growth) leads here. When you land on step four, you have reached a level of confidence where you look positively at the world and understand how energies work; that is, you understand that the energy you send out into the world is the energy that you will get back. What you radiate also determines which people are attracted to you, which groups and forums you fit into, and so on.

There is an old Swedish proverb that says "equal children play best." I understand this to be about energies, because humans are all energy and transmit on different frequencies, either low or high. In the image you also see a red and a blue horizontal line. Red represents the level you fall to if something happens that you are mentally unprepared for. You can face a situation and be forced to make a super-fast decision, standing with your back to the wall, feeling extremely stressed! Automatically, all redundant systems are disconnected from your body because stress takes so much energy. "Panic" mode sets in. This is step one of the stairs—Survival. No good decisions are made on the first step because awareness is at zero.

You never want to end up here.

The blue horizontal line—Set Point Mode—represents the level you fall to under stress. This can happen even if you have reached the fourth step, Confidence. A person who has a higher degree of awareness and has gone through themselves, cleaned out what does not serve them, and reached a confident level does not fall as deep. This person has tools to control the thoughts and direct his energy so that they can still act rationally under stress. Of course, there is no rule without exception, but the truth is that the more you have developed your inner qualities, the better you feel about yourself and the better prepared you are for emotional events such as stress. You are already in a holistic approach, and even if this field of vision shrinks under stress, it will not shrink as much as it does for those who have never developed their inner self.

Set Point Mode is the foundation on which you should rest. Your frequency and vibration should start here, and not lower.

And just think—everything is connected with your self-confidence!

One's approach to The Confidence Stairs naturally varies depending on which step one is on, or which they are heading towards. You can come from Survival and be on your way up the stairs, and then you have a different way of thinking from the beginning.

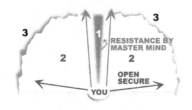

1. NARROW VIEW
2. THE CONFIDENT VIEW
3. NEW DEVELOPMENT

WHAT IS INSIDE OF YOUR MASTER MIND?
WHAT KIND OF RADIATION WILL YOU PERFORM?

Model by Ki is your host.

1. **The Narrow View – Red Line:** This line demonstrates how we often think when we are afraid or insecure, and how we do not see our surroundings. If we were to raise our gaze, we would soon think of something negative that we have encountered, and quickly bounce back into the red narrow line with a limited field of view. It is the stored events and unpleasant memories in our Master Mind that come back to us; a so-called "resistance by Master Mind." We are reminded, and we adjust ourselves back to our old patterns. This is why it is so important to let go of what does not serve us, to identify these thoughts and get rid of them. Otherwise, they may chase us all our lives.

This affects the charisma you have towards the outside world, and how you are perceived. This is an area that you want to direct yourself!

2. **The Confident View – Blue Line:** This line represents an open way of thinking where you are fearless and confident. In this state, you do not limit yourself, but you take in a holistic view. It makes you safer because you overlook and take in your surroundings and what is happening in it.

   On the second step of The Confidence Stairs model, you will find different specializations. This is the one that is stagnant, and the one that wants to be further developed to achieve The Confident View, which also means climbing higher up the stairs.

3. **New Development:** The more fearless you are and the more you open your senses, the easier it is to see new opportunities. These usually occur outside of regular patterns. If you think about it, the term "development" actually implies reaching or achieving something new; if you have seen it before, it can hardly be called development.

Of course, this image interacts with what we talked about earlier, The Master Mind and your inner self. This determines where you are on the stairs. But remember, it does not matter where you come from if you are heading in the right direction. Whoever you are and whatever you have been through, you can change your situation and live your life to the fullest—the way you want to live. It just comes down to how you use your power of thought.

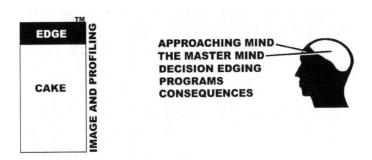

Model by Ki is your host.

If The Master Mind is the storage center, the Approaching Mind is the director. Take control and activate the director within yourself! Increase your awareness!

It is important that you choose the right company, because you should want to surround yourself with people who are open. You may have heard children being told who to play with, and which gangs are not good to hang out with, etc. This applies not only in childhood, but throughout your entire life! You need to surround yourself with positive energy, not negative energy that will pull you down. Be careful which friends you keep close.

In my eyes, change is something absolutely fantastic that makes life more fun. It is change that has given me many new opportunities.

How do you feel about change? And why do you feel that way?

Creating things or coming up with new ideas during instances of change also strengthens self-confidence. What can happen if your idea is crazy or weird? Nothing, except the fact that you add a creative value to yourself that can be very important!

> *"Creativity is intelligence having fun."*
>
> — Albert Einstein

If you are looking at change, look upon it with open eyes. Anything can happen or be served through change. Is there something I'm good at that can fit in? Which actors are involved in the events where the change takes place? Is there something that I can add here? Which companies are interested in the change?

Are there seminars or lectures I can attend to learn more?

How can I get involved in any of these?

How can I gather positive people around me and share my thoughts? Who are the positive people that I know already?

As you can see, those thoughts are very forward-moving and driven, and it is important that they be that way. Nothing bad can happen. There is nothing to be afraid of; it's just changing your mindset. On the contrary, change and development are great fun, interesting and exciting. Sometimes you may find that you lack the skills in a certain area that you are interested in. In that case, you should try to obtain the skills that are needed. Talk to the right authorities and plan how to obtain those skills and make the move from A to B. The person who is active and driven—the person with positive thoughts—will succeed. It's important to remember that this change is not a "quick fix." Rather, it is about continuously training yourself to think in the right way. It is training that brings on the skill, and things will be exactly as you want them to be if you are disciplined in your training. If this idea seems overwhelming, start by sitting at home in the house and writing down your plans.

Your thoughts are the strongest parts of you; they are your own, and no one else can control them. You can do whatever you want with your thoughts, and as a result, you can do anything you want with your life!

That's the beauty of building self-confidence…you're not dependent on anyone else being yourself. No one else can put sticks in your wheel, and the more experiences you go through, the smarter you will become.

Pressure makes diamonds. All the things you go through make you a wiser person. And you have to use this, because experience is a very good teacher. Analyze the events and think!

The other day I was talking to one of my closest friends who was very surprised about a particular circumstance. "I learned so much in a single day," he said. He had been involved in a fundraiser whereby he knocked on about sixty doors. Fifteen had opened their doors, but only two had invited him into their home. Afterward, he thought, "That's exactly how life is." If you stop after thirty doors, you will never reach the fifteen that would open for you, and of course, you'd never reach the two who welcomed you inside. The one who always stops after thirty doors will never reach their goals in life.

Imagine going through life and never achieving what you really want! This cannot happen!

I thought about this for a while. It was so wisely reasoned that I decided I had to include it in this book. It's about endurance. It's about having 100% certainty that we can all get exactly where we want to be, if and only if we have the endurance to get there.

I once read a story in a newspaper about why there are so relatively few millionaires in the world compared to those who are not rich. Leaving aside the poverty that prevails in some parts of the world, the second reason for the distance between the wealthy and the non-wealthy is *endurance*. Most people stop after only thirty doors, so they never reach those that would have been opened to them further down the line. Some give up right in front of the finish line without knowing that they were only a short distance from success.

I cannot stress enough the importance of never giving up!

You can get exactly what you want in your life if you think right and move forward regardless of the circumstances. Having discipline and endurance makes all the difference!

The same applies when building confidence. You must continue your efforts without stopping, and if you do, you will succeed. There is no one who has failed when they have continued forward with discipline and awareness. Without awareness, discipline and belief, yes, you will fail.

Many people have difficulty with the aspect of time. *When will it finally happen?* You want to know a timeline, but it does not work that way. Different people require different amounts of time to take control of their own thoughts and drive the development of their inner selves. You are on a journey that continues throughout life. The journey becomes easier and easier with time, and with more awareness you build within yourself.

> *"Time is an illusion."*
>
> — Albert Einstein

I have always been involved in mental training, but never before on the spiritual level as I am now. It took me just over eight months of training every day before it slowly started to work. I was determined to keep going until I got the results I wanted, and this started to show more and more. Sometimes I failed and fell into a pit, but I got up again and kept pushing forward. After these eight months, my success has continued in forward-moving momentum. I am still on my journey, still knocking on doors, and looking forward to the future progress as I encounter more doors that will be open to me. In truth, I know they have already been opened. It's just a matter of reaching them and walking through. I live in that thought now—that I have already walked through these doors. Now I must make some wise decisions.

Chapter Five

Awareness

We are all energy; therefore, we can control our emotions to different frequencies by focusing our thoughts. It is not any more complicated than that, but as I mentioned, it requires that you practice it. When building up your self-confidence, it is just as important to shut out bad energy as it is to let in energy that will strengthen you. We have talked about how this choice is made in the Approaching Mind.

The bad energy carried by people who pull you down should be shut out. Most importantly, you do not need these people's validation or approval for anything at all.

The image below shows your energy field radiating towards a goal or a desire that you want to achieve. You radiate out the sum of the climate inside of you, and the mindset that lives in you.

Model by Ki is your host.

1. **GOAL**: The direction you are moving; where you are heading.

2. **PEOPLE**: Surround yourself with people who are on the same frequency and who have similar energies to yours. These people probably share your drive and your passion to achieve established goals. When your frequencies are aligned, you work well together.

3. **MISMATCH**: Do not chase people who are on another frequency. If you are open, you will also feel that you are not syncing with them. It will be difficult to steer those people towards the goal, to support you, or to have an exchange in the way you would like.

There is more than one style that fits everyone, and not everyone fits every style. This is natural. Who do you "vibe" with? Think about it carefully.

"Energy cannot be created or destroyed, it can only be changed from one form to another."

— Albert Einstein

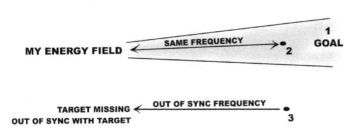

Model by Ki is your host.

Above, you can see different frequencies and the people within them. Many people do not know that they are placed here in relation to you or where they want to go, and that makes them lose ground. Remember that it is your thoughts and how they are directed that decides what frequency you are in—high or low.

From my experience, so many things become easier when I begin to observe and identify that the people around me are actually in different frequencies depending on whether they carry positive or negative energy charges. Remember that a "closed" person cannot identify this because the "closed" person has not examined himself or herself. That person can make all sorts of misjudgments. This truth can have serious consequences if, for example, this person is a recruiter in a company. It is not uncommon for this to be the case.

Earlier in life, I often thought, "This might not be the perfect situation, but I will try to work with this person anyway." I felt that it was not optimal, but unfortunately, I did not trust my own gut feeling. In retrospect, when I have immersed myself in my own development, I clearly see the mistakes I made with some people I encountered. I now understand that we did not sync with each other—we were not on the same frequency.

Now that I am more aware, having reached a whole new level of awareness, everything suddenly seems so clear. I "know" which people will not bring positive thoughts to the relationship, and I consciously avoid allying myself with them. It has changed my life because I have released that which does not serve me.

To do this, however, you need to be aware of it. You need to feel and see it, experience it. The way to get there is through training your inner strengths and awareness. Sadly, the majority of the people in this world are not aware, and therefore it is very important that you be in charge of your own navigation. People use only a small percentage of their brain and their thinking power, which is quite telling.

These are again thoughts about how unaware many people are. You want to belong in the group with those who are aware; this will give you everything you want in your life.

Chapter Six

Be Prepared to Take Action!

Preparing yourself by putting yourself through scenario-based training is important. Becoming familiar with a scenario before it occurs means that you recognize the situation, and will thus be more comfortable when it arises in real life. Self-confidence grows in conjunction with this preparation, because we normally feel much more insecure when experiencing something we have never experienced before.

Market guru Napoleon Hill claimed as early as the 19th century that there are no failed meetings or situations—only failed preparations. Let that be food for thought.

Why do people fail in certain situations? Did you fail because you did not know what to do? Or did you fail because you were not prepared? If you did not know what to do, you must have been careless before the meeting!

This is also related to how you want the environment to perceive and look at you. Are you the one who is always comfortable in meetings and among friends? Are you professional and collected?

Or is that what you *want* to be?

You can be that person if you plan ahead, and if you imagine all the possible scenarios that may occur and see yourself acting in them. All this preparation takes place in your own thoughts.

The opportunities for you to achieve what you want are real—and they are fantastic!

This entire book has been about the power of thought. No matter how we twist and turn the reasoning, it is always the power of thought that makes itself present in all aspects. It is particularly important and necessary that you are not dependent on anyone else when you build your new confidence. You are only dependent on your own thoughts! Remember that confidence is not something that can be learned like a set of rules; confidence is a state of mind. It's how you feel and what energy you radiate out.

There are those who say that confidence and self-esteem are not the same thing, but the reason I did not make a distinction between them in this book is that I think the two are intertwined and must be managed as a single component. I want to see it a little more holistically.

We have spent a lot of time talking about how to build your inner self, but the outer self is also important: your posture, gestures, and how you stand when you talk to other people, for example. Of course, the fact that we straighten our backs a bit when feeling confident is a natural element, but it's still something we must be aware of. If you want to be successful, you can also practice having a confident body.

Stand in front of the mirror. It may feel weird at first, but you get used to it soon. I have stood in front of the mirror for hours before stage performances and speeches. Does this particular gesture look confident and bring emphasis to these words? Is it a powerful enough gesture? What is the feeling I want to create in the mind of the recipient?

It is all about giving the audience or the group that special *feeling*.

We talked earlier about how we can psychologically influence our surroundings, and this is one such opportunity. There are several examples of how we, with our thoughts and gestures, can spread such a powerful aura around us that we gain the respect and interest of others. There are also other times when we may need to build confidence in something we want to push through, or when we need to consolidate our position as a leader.

The truth is that the message is not the focus, but rather, the focus is on the person who conveys the message. It's the feeling that is radiated from us, and the credibility that we succeed in conveying. Again, it is about our mindset.

Picture by Ki is your host.

The picture with the stick figures shows: a) a winning attitude; and b) a person who will not gain confidence. Openness and having welcoming open arms make people who see you feel lighter and more secure because they see that you are secure. Arms close together and closed against the upper body create a completely different atmosphere. It is difficult to gain confidence in a person who does not convey open behavior in, for example, a leadership role. It is the same in all situations. Somehow, this is a vicious circle. If you feel depressed and insecure, it is difficult to enter the room with open arms and a positive outlook. When you then close yourself off because you are not confident or don't have good self-esteem, the effect of being a closed person is enhanced.

That's why practicing in front of the mirror is so ingenious. Smile to yourself, stretch yourself, open your arms in a welcoming and safe gesture. Now do it again, and again! Then you can try this in front of your family, or someone you trust who wants to support you in your self-development work.

This practice works even if it feels ridiculous at first. I often look at myself in the mirror, and the person looking back at me becomes more and more beautiful with time. Yes, attitude comes from within and is an important ingredient when it comes to having a psychological impact on your surroundings.

I can take an example from my time as a fitness coach for elite teenage male athletes. We had a new player in the team, a big strong guy who was also a bit cockier than the rest of the team. The first time he confronted me was during a gathering where I was to instruct the team. He started fussing with me from his place where he sat on the table, his big shoes placed on the bench.

I knew I had to act fast. I went straight to him and stared right into his eyes while I calmly rebuked him. I stood so close to him that I could almost see his thoughts moving around behind the forehead bone. He did not understand anything, and he was completely stunned.

A female leader, half the size of himself, standing far too close for comfort and staring straight into his brain! He looked away, and one of the other players quickly reprimanded him. It would not have happened if I had acted differently, or more slowly, but it is important to use different maneuvers in different situations. This time it was about attitude. Consider these scenarios in advance.

For better or worse (but almost always), I have been fast in these situations. As I stated in Chapter 2, "attack mode" is often the best defense. However, you must always assess your surroundings before acting. Different atmospheres require different handling, which is why you need to prepare in advance in order to win in any situation.

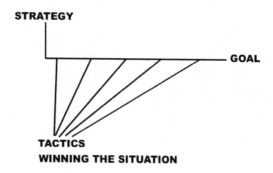

Model by Ki is your host.

I have used the model above to support refugees in building their self-confidence after arriving in their new homeland. It is not so easy when you do not know how to act, because there are often major cultural differences. In these situations, it is important to be prepared and have a good model as a foundation of support and source of direction. I will describe what the picture contains.

GOAL: Start by deciding the goal you want to achieve. In this case, it may be to achieve confidence—but you can use this model for any goal you set for yourself. Goals are extremely important, both the short- and long-term. You may not know immediately how to achieve it, but it will become clear during the journey and the more you use your thinking power to plan.

STRATEGY: What is your long-term strategy? What do you want to achieve? A life change? Something else that is more concrete...maybe buying a new home? Strategy means that you know where you want to go, and you lay a path to get there—a plan.

TACTICS: On the path toward the goal when following your strategy, you will pass several events with situations that you want to "win." It could be forums you participate in, it could be people you meet, or anything else you come across. For every situation you may encounter, you need a tactic to guide you in knowing which approach you should take. It could be having certain words ready to say, or it could be acting in a certain way—both of these require preparation.

Remember Napoleon Hill's words about failed meetings: they do not exist. What exists is bad preparation, and it's terribly unnecessary!

WINNING THE SITUATION: This simply means that we win every situation on our path toward the goal. The more we prepare and win individual situations, the more we build ourselves up. As a result, our drive toward the goal becomes stronger.

Below you see a picture of "scenario training." It is good to combine with "winning the situation." Each situation, event, or plan can result in several different potential scenarios.

SCENARIO TRAINING

Model by Ki is your host.

"Scenario training" is a practice whereby you write down all potential scenarios that can happen in a situation that you will face. This could be an interview, a meeting with a group of people, or anything else that you will possibly be involved in. Mark them 1, 2, 3, and so on.

For each one, you need to also write a description of the participants in the potential scenario, the surroundings, and finally your own actions and solutions.

What action will benefit you?

> "If you want to live a happy life, tie it to a goal, not to people or things."
>
> — Albert Einstein

This is a simple but very useful exercise, and it helps you to walk more confident into each meeting or circumstance knowing you can "win the situation." It is not complicated. When you are prepared for what can potentially happen, you walk in with more confidence and the stress dissipates because you are prepared. You have been there before (in your thoughts), so it is real! Of course, there are always unexpected things that can happen in life, but scenario training almost works without fail by nearly performing a miracle on a person's mind.

One last thing that we need to add to our efforts in building confidence is self-motivation.

Self-motivation, at its simplest, is the force that drives you to do things. However, self-motivation is not simple. At any given moment, there are likely to be different forces driving your behavior, and they are likely to vary in strength depending on your mood and what has happened that day.

We need to understand that life has its ups and downs. Sometimes we will be stronger, and sometimes we will be weaker, but how we motivate ourselves and how we handle our tools will determine our outcomes. You can build yourself to be very strong and deal successfully with negative events that you may encounter. I am often asked how one should inspire and motivate oneself, and the answer is really quite simple:

You should do what you love!

We all have something that we are passionate about, and that is what we should do, because immediately afterward we are happy and inspired. To motivate ourselves, we need to have goals that we are passionate about. If we do not have such a thing, we must seek them out from our inner being and ask ourselves what we really want, what we love, and what we are happy about. Stop and think!

Motivation always comes from what we are passionate about, and it will come much easier when we first let go of those things that do not serve us. It all starts with relieving the burdens that trouble us. Then the door is open to motivation, joy, and a light that will change our lives.

Chapter Seven

Step by Step Process to Confidence

Below is a simple process that you can complete, and like Albert Einstein, I would like to remind you that time is an illusion. You should not focus on time. Forget "time." How long or short it will take for you to reach the level of confidence you want to be at is different for each person. The important thing to remember is to promise yourself that you will move forward and work with this process no matter how long it takes. The one who is disciplined and to the letter completes his program will succeed. I have not met a single disciplined person who has failed. The law of attraction works 100% for those who bet it all!

So, do you now understand that the foundation of your self-confidence is your ability to control your own thoughts?

It's your ability—no one else's!

What others think does not have to affect you if you are strong in your own faith. Sounds good, doesn't it? You only need to change one thing: your thoughts. You can completely control yourself without being dependent on anyone else. Isn't that wonderful? You are not dependent on anything else, or anyone, to succeed; it is your own thoughts that you must properly control—that's all!

Here is a process that works if you give it 100% discipline and commitment. Start from number 1 and continue.

1.   AWARENESS

Model by Ki is your host.

Become aware of your inner self—your Master Mind—and release anything that does not serve you. Identify attachment to meaning. Look at history. Who are you? Do you have a blueprint of the outcomes and reality? Identify your attachment style: Confident, Anxious, Resisting, or Neutral.

Do you need to take action?

Let go of meaning. Meaning gives all the power and energy to the situation or to the person that you give this meaning to, and that puts you in a position of being in need.

Change the meaning, and you will change your life.

Make sure you understand the following concepts:

1. the past
2. the present
3. the future

Take a walk through all of the models in this book and create one that you will fill in for yourself.

Meditation – Part 1

Find a good method of meditation to raise your vibration. Let go of what does not serve you. Maybe the theme of your meditation should be to simply let go of meaning. There are many incredibly good meditations on YouTube. Pick one that is around 15-40 minutes long, and start EVERY morning with this meditation BEFORE you get out of bed.

Breathing is important. Keep your awareness on your breath, as this will help you to focus. Your full attention must be on your body when breathing. From now on you will start living from your heart.

2. MY GOAL

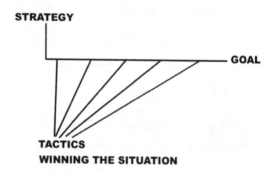

Model by Ki is your host.

1. Identify the feeling – set the GOAL. What do you want?

2. Establish the feeling – accept the goal as possible.

3. Practice the feeling – live in the goal as if you have already achieved it.

SCENARIO TRAINING

Model by Ki is your host.

Use your scenario training and think ahead about every task or every situation that you are going into.

Meditation – Part 2

Add your own moment of gratitude for 10-15 minutes immediately following the meditation Part 1. Now is the time to be thankful for everything you have, for reaching your goal and already living it. Use this time to send love to other people and to the universe that you trust 100%, just as you trust yourself.

If you are not already training your body, set aside a time each day (or at least 3-4 times weekly) where you perform any physical exercise of your choice. Pay attention to what you eat, and try to eat healthy most of the time.

3. LOVE YOURSELF

Do things that you are passionate about!

With a daily commitment of around 30 to 60 minutes each morning, you should be set and ready. Remember to stay on track even though times can be rough. Discipline is key. You must be 100% committed, no matter how you feel that day.

There will come days when you feel extra tired, but nothing should stop you from doing your morning meditation, your moment of gratitude, and boosting your goals!

Good luck. You are so much stronger than you think!

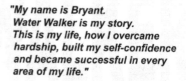

"My name is Bryant.
Water Walker is my story.
This is my life, how I overcame
hardship, built my self-confidence
and became successful in every
area of my life."

WATER
WALKER

The inspiration behind the confidence models in Walk Tall!

Coming in 2022!
www.waterwalker.online

FREE DOWNLOAD!

**GET THE TOP 3 THINGS TO DO
AND THE BEST AFFIRMATIONS
TO ACHIEVE RESULTS!**

GET IT HERE:
www.kiisyourhost.com

Let´s do it!

Thank you for reading! If you enjoyed this book or found it useful, I would be grateful if you could post a short review on Amazon. Alternatively, if you purchased this book via www. kiisyourhost.com, you can email your review. Your support really does make a difference. I read all reviews personally so I can use your feedback to make the next book even better.

Thanks again for your support!

*"Dream the impossible and speak it
into existence."*

— Lewis Hamilton,
Formula 1 Champion (on f1chronicle.com)

*"Any fool can know, the point is
to understand."*

— Albert Einstein

HEARTS to be HEARD

Giving a Voice to Creativity!

With every donation, a voice will be given to
the creativity that lies within the hearts of
our children living with diverse challenges.

By making this difference, children that may
not have been given the opportunity to have their
Heart Heard will have the freedom to create
beautiful works of art and musical creations.

Donate by visiting

HeartstobeHeard.com

We thank you.

9 781774 820421